"The *Yellow Roses* documentary is what so many young girls need to see. It doesn't shy away from hard issues but embraces the complexity and difficulty of teenage life. I love how the girls tell their own stories, in their own words. It's very real and honest, and the girls watching will feel that. *Yellow Roses* addresses these issues from a loving Christian perspective, when most messages teenage girls get about church are condemning or irrelevant to their lives. I look forward to sharing this film with many teenage girls and pray that the love of God will touch each one who watches it."

—STEPHANIE NEAL, case manager and small-groups leader,
Lower Lights Ministries, Campus Crusade for Christ

"*Yellow Roses* speaks of the struggles young women face today as well as the hope and healing they can find through an intimate relationship with Jesus Christ. My husband and I work with youth and feel that this film will have a positive, practical use in our ministry. Girls will realize they are not alone in their insecurities and challenges and will see their own beauty and dignity as daughters of God."

—KIMBERLY HENKEL, former executive vice president, National Pro-Life Action Center;
youth worker, St. Vincent de Paul Catholic Church, Mount Vernon, Ohio

"This is exactly what our young ladies need. The curriculum offers great opportunities for discussion and growth, and the issues are real and pertinent to what our ladies face on a daily basis. I wish I'd had *Yellow Roses* earlier; however, I am looking forward to using it this year!"

—BETH HACKER, high school Bible teacher, Grove City Christian School

"This movie is jaw-dropping truth, as one pastor put it at the church where I presented it. I highly recommend this film to any youth pastor looking for relevant material for students."

—ANNE RICE, ʼncoln, Nebraska

STUDENT BOOK

Yellow Roses

Real Girls.
Real Life.
Real Hope.

SALLY D. SHARPE

TH1NK, an
Imprint of
NavPress

NavPress is the publishing ministry of The Navigators, an international Christian organization and leader in personal spiritual development. NavPress is committed to helping people grow spiritually and enjoy lives of meaning and hope through personal and group resources that are biblically rooted, culturally relevant, and highly practical.

**For a free catalog go to www.NavPress.com
or call 1.800.366.7788 in the United States or 1.800.839.4769 in Canada.**

CONTENTS

HOW TO USE THIS STUDY

You are part of a generation of young women weighed down by pressures greater than any previous generation has had to face. The destructive impact of the media, society, and technology on your sense of self-worth is undeniable. The fact that you are a generation in turmoil is evidenced by higher-than-ever rates of depression, anxiety, eating disorders, self-mutilation, and even suicide. Yet, in the midst of all this disquiet, there is great hope!

In Victorian times, a yellow rose symbolized a new beginning. The purpose of *Yellow Roses* is to come alongside you and other young women as you struggle with the problems and pressures of life while offering the promise of a beautiful new beginning. Combining a full-length documentary film and a video-based group study, *Yellow Roses* introduces a refreshingly unique approach to ministry with young women that encourages open, honest sharing about the real issues and struggles you are dealing with on a daily basis.

It is relationship-based and conversation-focused. Leave your safe Sunday school answers at home and come prepared to be real. You'll appreciate the straightforward style that quickly gets down to the heart of the matter each week, helping you identify the lies the world wants you to believe. In week 1, you will meet a diverse group of young women who courageously reveal not only their confusion — and in some cases, the deep physical and emotional pain they have faced — but also the ultimate hope they now embrace. As you watch the *Yellow Roses* film, you will experience a strong connection with these young women who speak openly about their own struggles precipitated by the pervasive influence of media, technology, and peer pressure. Then, in weeks 2–8, you will encounter the stories of young women who, like you, are dealing with a variety of life and relationship issues, such as the pressure to perform, the struggle with body image and physical appearance, the pain of hurtful words and cyberbullying, the pitfalls of peer pressure and temptation, and the deep wounds of abuse. (If you need to refresh your memory later or want to learn more about the backgrounds of the girls in the stories, you can find the Real-Life Profiles on pages 109–114.) Each week as you talk together about these stories, you will have the opportunity to share how the same issues and topics are impacting your own life. Then, through video and group interaction, you will explore some timeless wisdom and encouragement related to these tough issues and how you can find forgiveness, hope, and healing.

At the end of the material for each week, you'll find a "Reality Check" of truth from God's Word, along with some memorable quotes. The "Reality Check" page is designed for you to tear or cut out and post somewhere you will see it often, such as the bathroom mirror, your dresser, the refrigerator, or your locker. The idea is to reflect and meditate on the verses throughout the week, allowing them to sink into your heart and mind. The tactic of the Enemy is to deceive and mislead us, but Jesus said that the truth will set us free (see John 8:32). We hope and pray that the truth will indeed set you free from the falsehoods that pervade our culture, enabling you to experience the new beginning God has planned for you: a future as beautiful and full of hope as yellow roses.

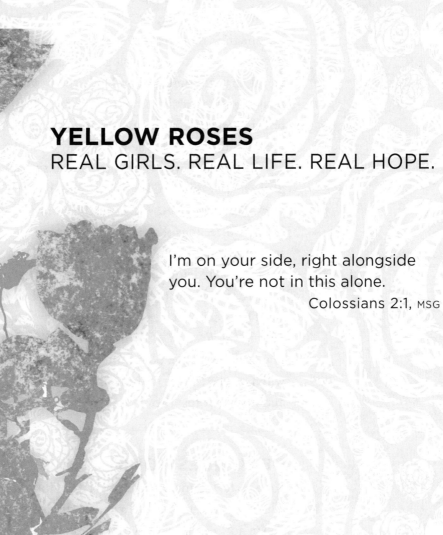

WEEK 1

YELLOW ROSES
REAL GIRLS. REAL LIFE. REAL HOPE.

I'm on your side, right alongside
you. You're not in this alone.

Colossians 2:1, MSG

REAL LIFE. REAL ISSUES.

"One person can handle only so much."

"I just feel like I have to be perfect."

"We so desperately want to fit in."

"We're all struggling with the same things."

These words were spoken by young women who are very much like you. They, too, live in a world far different from the one their mothers grew up in. They know what it's like to navigate life in this technologically driven, media-saturated world that continually bombards them with messages and images and expectations and pressures. They, too, find that how they feel about themselves and their lives is often at the mercy of their friends, the media, and technology.

Today you have the opportunity to sit back and observe as these and other young women courageously share their fears, their struggles, and even their most personal experiences and feelings. You will discover that, despite how you sometimes feel, you are not alone. And you will hear a message of redemption and restoration that will give you hope for facing the pressures and problems in your own life.

This week you'll be watching the full-length documentary *Yellow Roses: Real Girls. Real Life. Real Hope.* (approximate running time: 60 minutes). After the film, your group will have the chance to think about what you saw and heard and discuss it together.

REAL QUESTIONS

Take a few minutes to answer the following questions. Then, if you're meeting as a group, discuss them together. If you're not comfortable sharing your answers with the group, that's okay, but just know that the more you open up with each other, the more you'll be able to understand and support one another.

What you say to each other in your group is private and should be protected. The only time it's appropriate for something private to be shared without permission is if someone is in danger of hurting herself or others or is being hurt by another person. Talk to your group leader or a trusted adult if this is happening or you are unsure whether or not your friend needs help.

1. What is one thing from the film that really spoke to you?

2. Could you relate to the girls in the movie? Why or why not?

3. Do you feel you're enough (pretty enough, smart enough, talented enough, confident enough)? Why or why not?

4. How does technology add pressure to your life?

5. What pressures do you experience related to guys and relationships?

6. Do you ever pretend to have it all together when you're really dying inside? What scares you about being real about your pain?

7. Where do you find hope?

KEEPING IT REAL
You're Not Alone

Life is hard. Sometimes it seems like a battle, and there are casualties all around you to prove it.

8. In what ways does life seem like a battle for you right now?

Actually, there is an Enemy of your soul who would like nothing better than to convince you that you are cornered and all alone, helpless and hopeless. But don't believe it! Hear what God's Word says:

Stay alert! Watch out for your great enemy, the devil. He prowls around like a roaring lion, looking for someone to devour. Stand firm against him, and be strong in your faith. Remember that your Christian brothers and sisters all over the world are going through the same kind of suffering you are. (1 Peter 5:8-9)

Did you catch it? That last sentence means that you're not alone! Others are experiencing the very same kinds of troubles and problems you're experiencing, and that includes your Christian sisters and brothers! Whatever you might be going through, you're not the only one who has ever had your problem or felt the way you're feeling. There are plenty of others who understand your pain, and together you can stand firm and be strong.

9. Do you feel all alone as you face pressure, struggles, and pain? Read Ecclesiastes 4:9-12. What can you learn from these verses? Write down the names of one or two people you can confide in.

10. How does knowing you're not alone give you encouragement and strength?

REAL HOPE

Here are some suggestions to help guide your group prayer time. Be sure to share prayer concerns and pray for one another.

- Give thanks that you are not alone on your journey but have others to walk with you.
- Ask God to show you how valuable you are to Him and to help you accept that you are enough.
- Thank God that you do not have to be perfect—for Him or for anyone else.
- Pray to be more than what society wants you to be—to be what God wants you to be.
- Pray for guidance, wisdom, and strength for handling the pressures and problems in your life right now.

Use the following space to write down prayer requests so you can pray for each other throughout the week.

REALITY CHECK

Tear out and post this page in a place you will see it often — a mirror, the refrigerator, your locker — or carry it in your pocket. You can also scan this QR code with your phone so you can take these verses and quotes with you wherever you go.

    Meditate on the following verses to nourish your thoughts with truth. Try to memorize one or more verses that stand out to you.

Week 1 Reality Check

🌹 You are not alone; God is always with you.

- 🌹 Never will I leave you; never will I forsake you. (Hebrews 13:5, NIV)
- 🌹 Be sure of this: I am with you always, even to the end of the age. (Matthew 28:20)
- 🌹 I will talk to the Father, and he'll provide you another Friend so that you will always have someone with you. This Friend is the Spirit of Truth. The godless world can't take him in because it doesn't have eyes to see him, doesn't know what to look for. But you know him already because he has been staying with you, and will even be in you! (John 14:15-17, MSG)

🌹 We have each other.

- 🌹 Two are better than one. . . . If either of them falls down, one can help the other up. (Ecclesiastes 4:9-10, NIV)
- 🌹 A friend loves at all times. (Proverbs 17:17, NIV)

Walking with a friend in the dark is better than walking alone in the light. — Helen Keller

Friendship is born at that moment when one person says to another, "What! You too? I thought I was the only one." — C. S. Lewis

Friends are like bras: close to your heart and there for support. — Anonymous

WEEK 2

TOO MUCH PRESSURE!
THE PRESSURES YOUNG WOMEN FACE TODAY

The pressure has built up, like lava beneath the earth. I'm a volcano ready to blow.

Job 32:19, MSG

REAL LIFE. REAL ISSUES.

Begin by playing the group study video for week 2, "Too Much Pressure!" (approximate running time: 4 minutes).

It's great to be a young woman today. Now more than any other time in history, you have incredible opportunities before you. But you're also living under an incredible amount of pressure! The pressure comes at you from all sides: parents, friends, teachers, coaches, the media, and society in general. Everywhere you turn, you are expected to excel. You are expected to be . . .

kind

well-liked

pretty

intelligent

talented

confident

capable

competitive

savvy

successful

. . . while simultaneously living up to the unrealistic and highly sexualized media images of women that bombard you daily. Add in the reality that comes with living in a cyberworld (every move you make, every conversation you have, and every snapshot or detail of your life that you or others choose to share is instantly visible to the world) and you have a recipe for disaster.

The result? Increased rates of depression, anxiety, eating disorders, self-mutilation, violence, and suicide. In fact, one-fourth or more of all girls in the United States between the ages of ten and nineteen face one or more of these threats.[1]

Young women everywhere are crumbling under all the pressure — young women like Sarah . . .

Sarah is a very pretty girl, and everyone says she should do some modeling. People who meet her for the first time are often surprised to learn that she's also an athlete. Last year she helped take the girls' basketball team all the way to the state championship. To the other girls, Sarah seems to have it all: looks, athletic ability, great grades, and a hot boyfriend, Matt, who is the quarterback of the football team. But the truth is that she's nearing her breaking point under all the pressure.

Sarah's parents run their own business, a gift shop, and expect her to help out as much as possible despite her demanding basketball schedule. They also have high expectations of her academically, lecturing her about improving her GPA and ACT score (which are already high) so that she can get the best scholarships possible. The business is suffering due to the economy, and Sarah's parents need all the financial help they can get. Her father also tries to motivate her to stay on top of her game so that she will be able to receive a basketball scholarship and play college ball (more his dream than hers).

One day Sarah unloads on her best friend, Cassie, as they're doing homework together—a rare occasion because of her busy schedule. She talks about how her parents are always on her case and how even her coach has been yelling at her for letting her game slip. Lately it seems that no matter what she does, it's just not enough.

Cassie listens for a while and then tries to make Sarah laugh. She's always cracking jokes and trying to make everything okay with her friends. Cassie suggests they take a break from the books and see who's on Facebook. Sarah asks if first they can check out that clothing website Cassie's older sister says all the college girls are crazy about. Sarah has the night off Saturday, and she and Matt are going out. She's hoping to find some ideas that will help her put together a hot new look.

Cassie knows the real reason Sarah wants to wow Matt this weekend, and her name is Amber. Even Cassie has seen the way Matt has been eyeing Amber when he thinks no one else is looking. Because Cassie and Amber are friends, it's a delicate subject. But both Sarah and Cassie know that Amber doesn't ask for or want the attention. When Cassie says something about Amber, Sarah's eyes flood with tears. Sarah asks if she needs to lose a few pounds. It's a question she asks often, even though she's already on the slim side.

Cassie changes the subject and tells Sarah she has a great idea: She will fix Sarah's hair and makeup to look like that model they were admiring in a magazine earlier. Sarah's face brightens. That sounds like just the thing that could help her get Matt's attention this weekend.

Matt's pretty strong-willed and tries to intimidate Sarah sometimes, but she just can't bear the thought of losing him. She still feels that she needs Matt's attention, affection, and strength in order to be okay. Matt has been pressuring her for weeks to have sex. Even though she knows it would be wrong, it's getting harder and harder to say no. Besides, she thinks that if she says yes, maybe he will lose interest in Amber for good. Then at least one area of her life would be less stressful.

REAL QUESTIONS

Take a few minutes to answer the following questions. Then discuss them together.

1. Can you relate to Sarah in any way? Have you ever felt as though you were at your breaking point—about to lose it because of all the pressure?

2. If you were Sarah's best friend, what would you say to her?

3. What are the pressures in your life? Where do these pressures come from (who do you aim to please)?

4. In what ways have you felt the pressure to excel—to be and do more?

5. How have you felt the pressure to fit in? Do you feel that you do fit in? Why or why not?

6. Do you feel free to be who you really are — who God created you to be — or do you strive to meet the expectations of others?

7. Galatians 1:10 says, "Obviously, I'm not trying to win the approval of people, but of God. If pleasing people were my goal, I would not be Christ's servant." What does this verse mean in relation to your situation and pressures?

8. Read 2 Corinthians 4:8-10 and 1 Peter 5:7. How do these verses encourage you?

KEEPING IT REAL

Backpack of Burdens

Imagine that every morning when you get out of bed, you have to strap a heavy backpack on your back. From the time you get up until the time you go to bed, you are required to wear it. You can't take it off even for one minute. It's killing you, and you don't know how much longer you can stand it.

You might not wear a heavy backpack all day every day, but you do have a lot of weight on you! You're carrying around your own backpack of burdens: pressures and problems that are weighing you down and causing you to feel stressed out, overwhelmed, or even hopeless. Jesus wants to lighten your heavy load and give you rest. He said,

> Come to me, all of you who are tired and have heavy loads, and I will give you rest. Accept my teachings and learn from me, because I am gentle and humble in spirit, and you will find rest for your lives. The burden that I ask you to accept is easy; the load I give you to carry is light. (Matthew 11:28-30, NCV)

You don't have to carry heavy burdens by yourself!

Some of the pressures that are weighing you down are unnecessary, and you need to eliminate them—to stop carrying them around. By making different choices, you can get rid of a lot of unnecessary weight in your life.

9. What are some of the pressures you can eliminate from your life by making different choices? List them and then beside each, write the choice you will make to get rid of the pressure. (For example: "The pressure to live up to my siblings: I will spend more time reading my Bible and asking God to show me who He created me to be and what makes me unique from my siblings.")

Other pressures you have no control over—you can't eliminate them or make them go away—but you can choose how you will respond to them. Jesus wants to walk with you and help you carry your burdens, teaching you to handle pressures and problems through His wisdom, guidance, and strength.

10. List three pressures you can't make go away right now. Beside each, write what is being asked or required of you. Pray about each expectation this week, asking God to show you how to respond and who you can turn to for help. (For example: "Pressure: good grades. Expectation: get a high enough GPA for college and scholarships.")

The Bible says that the Enemy is a thief who wants to steal, kill, and destroy; his tactic is deception, trying to make you believe lies about yourself, others, and your circumstances (see John 10:10). The Enemy wants you to feel as though the weight of the world is on your back and there is no one to help you. But Jesus came so that you can have abundant life—a life that is rich and satisfying. He wants to walk with you and lighten your load. His plan is to give you a life that is full of peace and joy—a life better than you ever thought possible.

If you don't have a relationship with Jesus—if you haven't already trusted Him with your future—you can begin that life-changing journey today. All you have to do is invite Him into your life. Acknowledge how desperately you need Him—He already knows—and tell Him you're tired of trying to handle life on your own. The truth is that you can't handle it alone. Tell Him you want the abundant life He gives, and ask Him to walk with you from now on.

If you're interested in learning more about what it means to trust Jesus with your life and your future, go to pages 115–118 or scan this QR code.

REAL HOPE

Here are some suggestions to help guide your group prayer time. Be sure to share prayer concerns and pray for one another.

- Life is hard, full of problems and pressures, but you are never alone or without help. Praise God for His promise to be with you always, whatever you are dealing with or facing. Thank Him for the wisdom, guidance, strength, help, and hope He gives you.
- Ask God to assure you that you are "enough" — that you are valuable, priceless, and loved unconditionally.
- Ask God to help you feel free to be who He has created you to be, remembering that the only One you need to please is God.
- Ask God to give you wisdom and guidance in identifying choices you can make to eliminate some of the pressure in your life.
- Ask God to show you how to respond to pressures and problems in the right ways so that your load is lightened.
- Pray for those in your group who may not have a relationship with Jesus. Pray that He comes into their lives right now and that they allow Him to help carry their burdens.

Use the following space to write down prayer requests so you can pray for each other throughout the week.

REALITY CHECK

Tear out and post this page in a place you will see it often—a mirror, the refrigerator, your locker—or carry it in your pocket. You can also scan this QR code with your phone so you can take these verses and quotes with you wherever you go.

Week 2 Reality Check

Meditate on the following verses to nourish your thoughts with truth. Try to memorize one or more verses that stand out to you.

🌀 **Problems and pressures are part of life, but God promises to be with you.**

   🌀 We have troubles all around us, but we are not defeated. We do not know what to do, but we do not give up the hope of living. We are persecuted, but God does not leave us. We are hurt sometimes, but we are not destroyed. We carry the death of Jesus in our own bodies so that the life of Jesus can also be seen in our bodies. (2 Corinthians 4:8-10, NCV)

🌀 **God cares about you and wants to help you.**

   🌀 Give all your worries and cares to God, for he cares about you. (1 Peter 5:7)

   🌀 I look up to the hills, but where does my help come from? My help comes from the LORD, who made heaven and earth. He will not let you be defeated. He who guards you never sleeps. (Psalm 121:1-3, NCV)

🌀 **Jesus will help carry your burdens and lighten your load.**

   🌀 Come to me, all of you who are tired and have heavy loads, and I will give you rest. Accept my teachings and learn from me, because I am gentle and humble in spirit, and you will find rest for your lives. The burden that I ask you to accept is easy; the load I give you to carry is light. (Matthew 11:28-30, NCV)

🌀 **God's plan is to give you a full, satisfying life.**

   🌀 The thief's purpose is to steal and kill and destroy. My purpose is to give them a rich and satisfying life. (John 10:10)

   🌀 "I know what I am planning for you," says the LORD. "I have good plans for you, not plans to hurt you. I will give you hope and a good future. Then you will call my name. You will come to me and pray to me, and I will listen to you." (Jeremiah 29:11-12, NCV)

When you get into a tight place and everything goes against you, till it seems as though you could not hold on a minute longer, never give up then, for that is just the place and time that the tide will turn. —Harriet Beecher Stowe

WEEK 3

AIRBRUSHED ILLUSIONS
EXPOSING THE LIES AND REDEFINING YOUR WORTH

The Lord doesn't see things the way you see them. People judge by outward appearance, but the Lord looks at the heart.

1 Samuel 16:7

REAL LIFE. REAL ISSUES.

Begin by playing the group study video for week 3, "Air-brushed Illusions" (approximate running time: 5 minutes).

Body image and self-esteem are huge issues for young women today. One study reports that 53 percent of girls are unhappy with their bodies at age thirteen. By age seventeen, the number skyrockets to 78 percent.[1] Considering the barrage of unrealistic media images you encounter on a daily basis—not to mention cultural messages from every direction to be thin, chic, and ultra-sexy—it's no wonder that so many young women are struggling with this issue!

Take a look at these statistics:

- More than half of teen girls either are on a diet or think they should be.[2]
- Roughly 4 percent of teen girls have some kind of eating disorder.[3]
- By college age, 1 in 100 suffer from anorexia, 4.5 to 18 percent have a history of bulimia, and 15 percent have disordered eating of some type.[4]
- Plastic surgery procedures among teens have almost tripled from 1997 to 2005.[5]

Dieting, eating disorders, plastic surgery, obsession about physical appearance—these are some of the common responses to the cultural pressure to conform to a certain physical standard or image, and they result in discouragement, loneliness, depression, and illness. Comparing yourself to others, including unrealistic airbrushed illusions, is a destructive habit that can wreak havoc on both your self-esteem and your body.

Consider Taylor . . .

Taylor is about five foot five and just below normal weight for her height. Her boyfriend, Michael, has wondered how she can eat so much junk food without gaining weight. Taylor likes to read fashion magazines and dreams of being a model. If only she were taller—and thinner. She hides her binge eating and purging so well that no one—not even Michael or her parents—is on to her.

Taylor is dissatisfied with her looks. She has dyed her hair just about every color that comes in a box; right now it's mahogany brown. She doesn't have the money to buy designer clothes, but she can put consignment store clothes together to make an outfit that looks like it came right off the runway.

Even so, Taylor is never satisfied with how she looks. She's unhappy with her nose and wants to have plastic surgery. She knows a girl who got a nose job from her mom and dad as a graduation gift. Maybe she'll have her breasts enlarged too. She has read how more and more teenage girls are having that done.

No matter how hard she tries, she just can't seem to look like the fashion models she spends so much time studying. She thinks that if she were thinner, prettier, and more fashionable, people would like her better and pay more attention to her. As the middle child—with an older brother and a younger sister—she wishes she got more attention at home. Because her brother plays several sports and her sister has ongoing health issues, Taylor often feels ignored and alone. Even when she's with her parents, they seem to be preoccupied with other things and not really interested in her, so she spends most of her time with Michael. They've known each other since elementary school and go to the same church. Sometimes he and Taylor work out together.

No matter what she does or who she is with, Taylor feels she just doesn't measure up. She hides it well on the outside, but inside she's miserable.

REAL QUESTIONS

Take a few minutes to answer the following questions. Then discuss them together.

1. Do you think Taylor would be happier or more content if she lost some weight and had the plastic surgery? Why or why not?

2. Was there anything Nicole or Melanie said in the video that stood out to you?

3. Are you happy with yourself the way you are? Why or why not?

4. How would you complete the following sentence? If only I had _____, then _____.

5. To whom or what do you compare yourself or aspects of your life?

6. Why is comparing yourself to others destructive?

7. What does the world say about your identity (who you are)? According to the world, what makes you valuable (see 1 Samuel 16:7)?

8. On a scale of 1 to 10, with 1 being low and 10 being high, how confident are you? What would help you feel more confident?

9. What does God say about your identity? According to God, what makes you valuable (see Genesis 1:27; 1 Corinthians 6:19; Galatians 5:1; Ephesians 1:3-4)?

10. Read Psalm 139:13-14. Is it difficult for you to accept and celebrate who God created you to be? Why or why not?

KEEPING IT REAL

Don't Believe the Hype

How do you feel when you look through the pages of a beauty or fashion magazine? Be honest. Do you tend to feel better or worse about yourself? Or are you completely unaffected by what you see?

☐ I'm completely unaffected.
☐ I feel better about myself.
☐ I feel worse about myself.

If we're honest, most of us would admit that those computer-enhanced images of seemingly flawless models often make us feel inferior or insufficient in one way or another. It's hard to live up to airbrushed illusions, isn't it? The truth is that we simply can't because they aren't real!

They are a false reality created by a consumer-driven culture that wants us to be continually dissatisfied with ourselves so we will buy more products and clothes and services. It's a never-ending and extremely destructive cycle. There are two steps in breaking free from this cycle. The first is to stop believing the hype and recognize the lies.

11. How do the beauty, fashion, and entertainment industries create a false reality through media-driven marketing and advertising?

12. What are some of the lies you have believed as a result of the false reality promoted by these industries? List them here.

The agenda of the media-driven beauty, fashion, and entertainment industries is to conform us to the world's standard of what's beautiful, which makes us discontent with who God created us to be. The song "What's Beautiful," by Everlife, is about this very struggle. After acknowledging our discontent with what we see in the mirror and our desire to be someone else, they sing these words of hope:

> I'm slowly starting to break free
> Learning how to truly love who I was made to be [6]

The only way we can break free is to renew our minds with the truth of God's Word. This is the second step in

What's Beautiful

breaking free from the destructive cycle of trying to measure up to a false reality. God's Word actually changes how we see things and what we think. In the book of Romans, we read,

> Do not be shaped by this world; instead be changed within by a new way of thinking. Then you will be able to decide what God wants for you; you will know what is good and pleasing to him and what is perfect. (Romans 12:2, NCV)

As you read what God's Word says about who you are and how God sees you, you will literally be transformed—from the inside out. Now that's some kind of makeover!

13. Take a look right now at the truths in this week's Reality Check. If you don't have time to read all of them now, choose one in each category. How do these truths speak to the lies you identified in question 12?

14. Which truth do you have the greatest need to accept right now?

Take the time to soak in all of these truths this week. It will be the best beauty treatment you could ever have!

REAL HOPE

Here are some suggestions to help guide your group prayer time. Be sure to share prayer concerns and pray for one another.

- Ask God to reveal the lies you have believed about who you are and how you're supposed to look and act.
- Ask God to free your mind with His truth so that you can see, accept, and be the real you He created you to be.
- Ask God to help you stop playing the comparison game and be content with who you are.
- Pray for the ability to believe how much God loves you and how beautiful you are to Him.
- Ask for the wisdom, courage, and strength to focus more on inner beauty than outer beauty.
- Pray for God-confidence — confidence rooted in the reality of who you are in Christ.

Use the following space to write down prayer requests so you can pray for each other throughout the week.

REALITY CHECK

Week 3 Reality Check

Tear out and post this page in a place you will see it often—a mirror, the refrigerator, your locker—or carry it in your pocket. You can also scan this QR code with your phone so you can take these verses and quotes with you wherever you go.

Meditate on the following verses to nourish your thoughts with truth. Try to memorize one or more verses that stand out to you.

🌹 **True and lasting beauty comes only from a relationship with God.**

> 🌹 Charm is deceptive, and beauty does not last; but a woman who fears the Lord will be greatly praised. (Proverbs 31:30)

🌹 **What matters is not how you look on the outside but what you're like on the inside.**

> 🌹 What matters is not your outer appearance—the styling of your hair, the jewelry you wear, the cut of your clothes—but your inner disposition. Cultivate inner beauty, the gentle, gracious kind that God delights in. (1 Peter 3:3-4, msg)

> 🌹 The Lord doesn't see things the way you see them. People judge by outward appearance, but the Lord looks at the heart. (1 Samuel 16:7)

🌹 **God made you in an amazing and wonderful way.**

> 🌹 You made my whole being; you formed me in my mother's body. I praise you because you made me in an amazing and wonderful way. What you have done is wonderful. I know this very well. (Psalm 139:13-14, ncv)

🌹 **This is who you are in Christ:**

> 🌹 God's child, made in His image (see Genesis 1:27; John 1:12; Ephesians 1:5)
> 🌹 Chosen and dearly loved (see Ephesians 1:4,11; Colossians 3:12)
> 🌹 Loved unconditionally (see John 3:16; Romans 5:8; 1 John 4:10)
> 🌹 Forgiven (see Isaiah 43:25-26; Acts 3:19; Colossians 1:13-14; 1 John 1:9)
> 🌹 Right with God (see Romans 5:1,10; Colossians 1:20-22)
> 🌹 A new creation (see 2 Corinthians 5:17)
> 🌹 Blessed (see John 1:16; Ephesians 1:3)
> 🌹 Filled with the Holy Spirit (see Romans 5:5; 1 Corinthians 3:16; Ephesians 1:13; 2:22)
> 🌹 Set free (see John 8:32; Romans 8:2; Galatians 5:1)
> 🌹 Victorious (see Romans 16:20; 1 Corinthians 15:57; 1 John 5:4)

No one can make you feel inferior without your permission.

— Eleanor Roosevelt

Always be a first-rate version of yourself instead of a second-rate version of somebody else.

— Judy Garland

WEEK 4

LONGING FOR LOVE
LETTING GO OF FAIRY-TALE FANTASIES

God picked you out as his from the very start.

2 Thessalonians 2:13, MSG

REAL LIFE. REAL ISSUES.

Begin by playing the group study video for week 4, "Longing for Love" (approximate running time: 3 minutes).

God has placed within the heart of every woman — young and old — the longing to be loved. We yearn to know we are valued and cherished. We want to be desired — to be seen as beautiful. God gave us these longings so we would seek Him, the only One who can truly satisfy our desires. Yet our tendency is to look to guys to meet these needs. After all, that's what our culture encourages us to do. Just think about the movie plots and sitcom scenarios you've seen in the past six months, not to mention all the advertising that seems to suggest that your sole purpose in life is to be attractive to the opposite sex.

Many of us believe that if a guy finds us attractive and wants to be with us, then we really are beautiful, desirable, and worthy of love. But we don't need the approval or acceptance of guys in order to have value; we are already passionately desired, unconditionally loved, and inestimably valued by God.

The trouble starts when we embrace the lies of the world rather than God's truth — lies such as:

- You're not beautiful unless you are desired by a guy.
- A boyfriend makes you special.
- You're nobody without a guy in your life.
- Your worth is determined by what guys think of you.
- You can't be happy unless you're in a relationship.
- Sex is love.
- The most important thing in life is to find a man.
- A man will complete you (fulfill all your longings).

Do you know anyone who believes one or more of these lies or variations of them? Have you ever found yourself thinking these kinds of thoughts? Tomika and Kimberly have . . .

Tomika is outgoing and flirty with the guys, especially Derrick. She likes Derrick to take her out and show her a good time as a "friend with benefits," but secretly she wishes it would become something more. Each time they're together, she feels an even stronger connection with him, and she hopes that, in time, he will feel it too. She's longing for love and thinks she may have found it with Derrick.

Tomika doesn't realize that Derrick likes their arrangement the way it is. If anything, he wishes she would just chill out and relax, but lately she seems to be even more intense—and confusing. He's frustrated by all the mind games she seems to play with him, and her constant talking is getting on his nerves too. It's as if she's thinking out loud. When he tries to offer a solution for one of her problems, she just gets mad at him. He also gets the feeling that she's trying to control him, and he hates that.

Tonight as Derrick is driving Tomika home, she is quiet for a change. Already she's thinking about the next time she might see him. She doesn't want the night to end. As she stares out the window at the moon, she wishes she knew what Derrick was thinking. Actually, if she did, she would be crushed!

Derrick is wondering if it's time to move on to another girl at school—maybe someone like Kimberly. But he wonders if things would be any different. He has heard that Kimberly has been unhappy since her boyfriend broke up with her. Actually, she's miserable. She believes that if only she could find the right guy, her life would be great. She's envious of her friends who have boyfriends, and she's desperate to find someone.

Derrick doesn't know that she has been out with Carlos a couple of times and already has become physically intimate with him.

As Derrick pulls into Tomika's driveway, he leans over to give her a kiss. To him, it means thanks for tonight—nothing else. To her, it means so much more. When did she give her heart away?

REAL QUESTIONS

Take a few minutes to answer the following questions. Then discuss them together.

1. What problems do you see in Tomika and Derrick's relationship? If you were Tomika's friend, what advice would you give her?

2. What does Kimberly's desperation for a boyfriend tell you?

3. If you are dating or would like to date, what are your reasons for dating? What do you want out of a dating relationship?

4. Do you feel you need the attention and acceptance of guys in order to be valuable? Why or why not?

5. Do you feel pressure to have a boyfriend because so many other girls do? Why or why not?

6. Do you feel better about yourself and your life when you are in a relationship with a guy? Why or why not?

7. Do you think it's possible to have a relationship with a guy (other than friendship) without getting emotionally involved? Why or why not? How can getting emotionally involved be a dangerous thing?

8. Earlier we read that Kimberly and Carlos are becoming physically intimate. Read Song of Solomon 2:7, Ephesians 5:3, and Matthew 5:28. What is God's standard of purity? Why do you think God wants you to keep yourself pure, and what does this involve?

9. Read Proverbs 4:23. What does it mean to guard (protect) your heart?

10. Do you think it's harder to stick to standards of purity once your heart has become involved in a relationship? Do you think it's possible to have a sexual relationship before marriage without getting hurt? Why or why not?

KEEPING IT REAL
The Perfect Match

Cinderella is the quintessential fairy tale. The prince finds Cinderella's glass slipper after the ball and searches the countryside to find her: the only girl in the kingdom the shoe will fit. At last they find each other—their true love—and now all of their dreams have come true. They get married and live happily ever after.

How many Cinderella stories have you seen played out in real life? That's just not the way real life is. Even the very best of marriages have ups and downs, challenges and disappointments. God never intended for any man to fulfill your longing for love. God picked you out as His from the very start. His Son, Jesus, is your perfect match, the only One who can fill the hole in your heart and satisfy all your needs. That's why fairy-tale romances are merely fantasies.

11. What fairy-tale fantasies (lies) about guys and relationships have you believed? List them here. Why is it important to let go of these fantasies?

It isn't wrong to want to be loved by a guy, but realistically you probably won't find your future husband in high school. These are the years you are learning who you are. You are exploring your interests, gathering knowledge, and discovering how the world works. These are also the years you're learning who you are in Christ: what it means to be loved by Him and what His plans are for your future. It's pretty hard to know what you and God want for your life if you don't know who you are first. God's plan for marriage is a lifelong covenant relationship, an unbreakable commitment, modeled after and established upon God's love. God designed marriage to be a picture of His love for us and His commitment to us. That's why purity is so important to God: because His love is pure. Only when we allow God to satisfy our longing for love and we understand who He has created us to be are we able to have the kind of relationship with guys that God intends, both before and throughout marriage.

12. What do you think it means to become the right person before you look for the right person? Why is this important?

13. What happens when you look to a guy (or guys) to satisfy your longing for love?

14. Take a look at John 3:16, John 17:23, and Hebrews 13:5. What do these verses tell you about where you can turn to for love?

15. Why is it important to protect your heart and keep yourself pure before marriage?

16. How can creating a standard for the kind of guy you would consider dating and then establishing boundaries up front help you guard your heart and keep yourself pure?

17. What kinds of qualities, characteristics, and behaviors would you include in your standard for a guy you would consider dating (now or in the future)? To get started, take a look at these verses: Proverbs 7; 20:7; 24:1-2; Ephesians 4:31-32; 1 Timothy 5:1-4.

18. If you've already taken your physical relationship(s) too far, it's never too late to start over. What boundaries could you set to help keep yourself pure? (For example: "I won't have physical contact that I wouldn't feel comfortable doing in the presence of my grandparents.")

REAL HOPE

Here are some suggestions to help guide your group prayer time. Be sure to share prayer concerns and pray for one another.

- Pray to recognize and let go of the lies you have believed about guys and relationships.
- Acknowledge that God gave you the desire to be loved so you would seek Him and find fulfillment in Him. Pray for the ability to accept this truth, looking to God alone to satisfy your deepest needs and longings.
- Ask God to help you become the right person before you start looking for the right person, and pray for patience to wait on God's timing.
- Ask God to help you protect your heart and keep yourself pure until marriage.

Use the following space to write down prayer requests so you can pray for each other throughout the week.

REALITY CHECK

Week 4 Reality Check

Tear out and post this page in a place you will see it often—a mirror, the refrigerator, your locker—or carry it in your pocket. You can also scan this QR code with your phone so you can take these verses and quotes with you wherever you go.

Meditate on the following verses to nourish your thoughts with truth. Try to memorize one or more verses that stand out to you.

🌹 **God is wild about you!**

🌹 The king is wild for you. Since he's your lord, adore him. (Psalm 45:11, MSG)

🌹 **True love is found in God and comes from God.**

🌹 We love because he first loved us. (1 John 4:19, NIV)

🌹 **Your heart is fragile. Guard it well.**

🌹 Above all else, guard your heart, for everything you do flows from it. (Proverbs 4:23, NIV)

🌹 **God does not want you to awaken love until the time is right.**

🌹 Don't excite love, don't stir it up, until the time is ripe—and you're ready. (Song of Solomon 2:7, MSG)

🌹 **Sex outside of marriage is not the way to express love.**

🌹 Don't allow love to turn into lust, setting off a downhill slide into sexual promiscuity. (Ephesians 5:3, MSG)

🌹 **Self-control will keep you safe.**

🌹 A person without self-control is like a city with broken-down walls. (Proverbs 25:28)

🌹 **God promises to love you.**

🌹 I love you unconditionally. (see John 3:16; Romans 5:8)
🌹 I will never leave you. (see Hebrews 13:5)
🌹 I know every detail about you and I still love you. (see Matthew 10:30; John 3:16)
🌹 Whatever happens, you can never be separated from My love. (see Romans 8:35)
🌹 I desire to live with you forever. (see 2 John 2)

We don't want to get our value from guys. We don't expect them to fill the hole in our hearts only God should fill. We don't want to hand them our hearts. We need to view our hearts as a gift.

— Alyssa Barlow, BarlowGirl

WEEK 5

STIX N STONES
OVERCOMING THE PAIN OF HURTFUL WORDS

When you talk, do not say harmful things, but say what people need—words that will help others become stronger. Then what you say will do good to those who listen to you.

Ephesians 4:29, NCV

REAL LIFE. REAL ISSUES.

Begin by playing the group study video for week 5, "stix n stones" (approximate running time: 4 minutes).

"Sticks and stones may break my bones, but words can never hurt me." You probably said these words or heard them from someone else at one time or another when you were younger. If only they were true. The truth is that words can hurt. In fact, they can break your heart and crush your spirit. That's because words have great power. They can build up, or they can tear down.

When it comes to words that tear down and destroy, the technological world we live in seems to only make matters worse. It's bad enough to be hurt by words in person — the wounds can be deep and difficult to heal from — but it can be completely overwhelming when you feel that you have no escape from hurtful words. With text messages, e-mails, instant messages, blogs, websites, tweets, and social networks invading your life 24/7, there are more opportunities than ever for hurtful words to wound and harass you, making you feel you have nowhere to be safe. And if those words are on public display via the Internet, it can seem as if the whole world is watching, judging, and perhaps even hating you. That's how Krista felt . . .

Krista lives to dance. Correction: She lived to dance — until her teacher crushed her dream of becoming a professional dancer. One day when Krista was talking about dancing professionally, her instructor carelessly remarked, "You want to dance professionally? But you will never have the body of a professional dancer, Krista." In an instant, Krista's dream was shattered.

After that, Krista's self-esteem took a nosedive. Over the next several months, she struggled with body image and became obsessed with losing weight. She started skipping dance class—something she'd never done before—and eventually dropped out because she couldn't bear to face her dance instructor anymore. Slowly but surely, she began to slip into depression, withdrawing more and more into herself. She even quit taking care of herself. Her friends noticed the changes and tried to talk to her about it at first, but she wouldn't open up. After a while, it was just easier not to say much at all. One day at lunch, it occurred to Krista that even though she was sitting with her friends, she might as well have been sitting alone. No one seemed to understand or care.

A few days later, one of Krista's friends was chatting on Facebook with Lindsay. She mentioned Krista and how strange she had been acting. She told Lindsay that Krista had quit dance, was obsessed with losing weight, was letting herself go, and was hardly talking to anyone anymore. Then she said she thought Krista was losing it.

"Do you think she's going crazy?" Lindsay asked.

"IDK . . . maybe," was the reply.

Lindsay just couldn't keep this to herself. It was too good. A few minutes later, she had a new status update: "Let's play 'Who am I?'" Then she added the following comments beneath the status:

"I'm chubby."

"I'm trying to starve myself, but it's not working!"

"I'm a dance dropout."

"I look awful."

"I don't talk to anyone."

"I'm losing it."

By this time, several people had made comments. A few of them made wrong guesses, but a couple of others wrote, "Sounds like Krista" and "Is it Krista?"

Before long, someone added a bad photo of Krista from an old yearbook. Then someone else added a picture of a person wearing a straight jacket. People who didn't even know Krista started making comments about how messed up she was. Someone called her mental, and someone else suggested she might as well end it all.

Lindsay didn't remember that Krista was one of her 673 friends. She had added her more than a year ago when they were in the same group for a project in English class. Even though she never made her own posts or comments, Krista still got on Facebook just about every day and scrolled through the news feed. It was almost a form of self-torture because it made her feel even less connected to everyone. But she was totally unprepared for what she saw tonight. Tears rolled down her cheeks as she read the comments and looked at the pictures. And then her eyes locked onto those last words: "She might as well end it all." She couldn't get the thought out of her head.

Take a look at the following statistics about cyber-bullying. Do they surprise you? Would you have guessed the numbers to be higher? Lower?

- Thirty-eight percent of girls who go online say they've been harassed (for example, threatening messages, e-mails forwarded without consent, embarrassing photos posted without permission, rumors).
- Fifty-eight percent of all youth report that someone has said mean or hurtful things to them online.
- Forty-two percent of all U.S. youth have been bullied while online.
- Thirty-five percent of all youth have been threatened online.

- Fifty-three percent of those surveyed admitted they themselves had said something mean or hurtful to another person online.[1]

REAL QUESTIONS

Take a few minutes to answer the following questions. Then discuss them together.

1. As you think about all the circumstances of the story you just read, what do you think Krista should do about what her teacher said, and what should she do about the bullying happening on Facebook?

2. What are some of the pros and cons of communicating with cell phones, e-mail, social networking sites, and other forms of technology? Make two lists here.

3. When was the last time you hurt someone else with words? How did you feel?

4. Recall a time when someone wounded you with words. How did the words affect your thoughts, feelings, and actions?

5. What kind of words do you speak more often: words that build up or words that tear down?

6. What is slander? Why is lying and deceiving others destructive, both to individuals and to relationships?

7. Has someone ever pretended to be your friend but then talked about you behind your back? How did you respond? Would you do anything differently now?

8. What do you think makes someone quick to criticize or blame others? Read Matthew 7:1. How have you found this verse to be true in your own life?

9. Why do you think it's so hard not to be drawn into gossip? What can you do when people around you start gossiping?

10. Why do you think profanity and "trash talk" are so common today? Read Ephesians 4:29 and Colossians 3:8-10. According to these verses, why must we stop using ugly and hurtful words?

11. Recall a time when someone built you up or lifted your spirits with praise or encouragement. How did the words affect your thoughts, feelings, and actions?

KEEPING IT REAL

The Gossip Game

Do you remember the first time you played the gossip game? The first person whispers a statement in her neighbor's ear, and then she whispers it to the next person, and so on around the circle. The last person says the message out loud, and it's usually very different from the original message. The game shows how easily truth gets distorted and misunderstandings occur as messages pass from person to person.

A similar thing can happen when you use technology to communicate, whether you're texting, tweeting, communicating on a social networking site, or sending an e-mail. With all the abbreviations and textese, sometimes misunderstandings occur. Even if you can make out all the words, it can be easy to misunderstand the message because there are no body gestures, facial expressions, or voice inflections to give you the right context or meaning.

12. Have you ever sent or received a message that was misunderstood? What caused the misunderstanding?

Communicating through technology also creates distance. Sending a text is much more impersonal than talking face-to-face or on the phone. And sitting in front of a computer screen can make you feel detached or removed from whatever you're about to say in cyberspace. That's why most people are not as careful or sensitive about what they say — or share — via technology as they are in person. It's also what encourages some people to cross the line and engage in cyberbullying (hurting or embarrassing someone by sending texts or images via cell phones or the Internet).

13. Have you ever been hurt or embarrassed by someone who was careless, insensitive, or even cruel through cell phone or Internet communication? How did it make you feel?

14. Have you ever hurt someone else by being careless, insensitive, or even cruel through the use of technology? Why did you do it? How do you feel about it now?

Although there were no cell phones or computers in Jesus' day, Jesus' words apply to every form of communication we have today: "I tell you that on the Judgment Day people will be responsible for every careless thing they have said"

(Matthew 12:36, NCV). This includes every careless or cruel word you've ever texted, posted on Facebook, or sent in an e-mail. If that sounds a bit extreme, remember that our words have great power. When God created the heavens and the earth, He used the powerful tool of words: "The LORD merely spoke, and the heavens were created. He breathed the word, and all the stars were born" (Psalm 33:6). And when God created human beings in His image, He gave us this same powerful tool. With our words, we have the power to bring life or death: "What you say can mean life or death. Those who speak with care will be rewarded" (Proverbs 18:21, NCV).

Every time you speak, you have a choice: Will you speak life or death? The apostle Paul encouraged us with these words: "When you talk, do not say harmful things, but say what people need—words that will help others become stronger. Then what you say will do good to those who listen to you" (Ephesians 4:29, NCV).

God wants you to build others up with your words, not tear them down. To make this choice every time you open your mouth, you will need the help of the Holy Spirit—God's Spirit living in you. Renew your mind daily with the truths in this week's Reality Check, and ask the Holy Spirit to give you the power to control your tongue.

15. With the help of the Holy Spirit, what changes do you want to make in the way you communicate with others?

REAL HOPE

Here are some suggestions to help guide your group prayer time. Be sure to share prayer concerns and pray for one another.

- Pray for healing from the wounds others have caused you with their words.
- Ask God to forgive you for the wounds you have caused others with your words.
- Pray about admitting your actions and asking the person or people you've hurt for forgiveness.
- Express your desire to turn away from all deception and lying, and ask God to fill you with the Spirit of Truth.
- Ask the Holy Spirit to help you tame (control) your tongue.
- Ask God to help you replace gossip, slander, criticism, and blaming with prudence, empathy, encouragement, and praise.
- Pray for the ability to use your words carefully and responsibly, always building up rather than tearing down.

Use the following space to write down prayer requests so you can pray for each other throughout the week.

REALITY CHECK

Tear out and post this page in a place you will see it often—a mirror, the refrigerator, your locker—or carry it in your pocket. You can also scan this QR code with your phone so you can take these verses and quotes with you wherever you go.

Meditate on the following verses to nourish your thoughts with truth. Try to memorize one or more verses that stand out to you.

Week 5 Reality Check

🌹 **Your words have great power.**

🌹 What you say can mean life or death. Those who speak with care will be rewarded. (Proverbs 18:21, NCV)

🌹 **Use your words to build others up, not tear them down.**

🌹 Encourage each other and build each other up, just as you are already doing. (1 Thessalonians 5:11)

🌹 When you talk, do not say harmful things, but say what people need—words that will help others become stronger. Then what you say will do good to those who listen to you. (Ephesians 4:29, NCV)

🌹 **An uncontrolled tongue brings destruction.**

🌹 It only takes a spark, remember, to set off a forest fire. A careless or wrongly placed word out of your mouth can do that. By our speech we can ruin the world, turn harmony to chaos, throw mud on a reputation, send the whole world up in smoke and go up in smoke with it, smoke right from the pit of hell. (James 3:5-6, MSG)

🌹 **Careless words have eternal consequences.**

🌹 I tell you that on the Judgment Day people will be responsible for every careless thing they have said. (Matthew 12:36, NCV)

🌹 **The more carefully you choose your words, the better they will be received.**

🌹 The right word spoken at the right time is as beautiful as gold apples in a silver bowl. (Proverbs 25:11, NCV)

The real art of conversation is not only to say the right thing at the right place but to leave unsaid the wrong thing at the tempting moment. — Dorothy Nevill

PEER-PRESSURE PUSHOVER?
SAYING NO WHEN EVERYONE ELSE IS SAYING YES

No test or temptation that comes your way is beyond the course of what others have had to face. All you need to remember is that God will never let you down; he'll never let you be pushed past your limit; he'll always be there to help you come through it.

1 Corinthians 10:13, MSG

REAL LIFE. REAL ISSUES.

Begin by playing the group study video for week 6, "Peer-Pressure Pushover?" (approximate running time: 3 minutes).

"But everyone does it!" Have you ever said these words to your parents or perhaps to a teacher or some other authority figure? If you're like most young women between the ages of thirteen and twenty-three, what your friends do and think are very important to you. In fact, your friends are huge influences in your life right now. That is a wonderful thing when they are encouraging you to do good things. The problem is that sometimes—whether knowingly or unknowingly—friends can encourage or influence you to do things that are wrong, unwise, or even harmful. That's when it becomes necessary for you to take a stand and say no.

Saying no isn't always easy, is it? Sometimes it feels like there's a battle raging inside you and you're torn between doing what you know is right and what your friends are doing. That's how Taylor felt when Melissa and Lindsay started pressuring her . . .

Melissa and Lindsay often go shopping together on Saturday afternoons. Melissa's mom gives her more spending money than she needs, and she is always generous to share it with Lindsay. One Saturday a couple of months ago, Melissa, who is a thrill seeker and enjoys taking risks, decided it would be fun to shoplift something. She started with a pair of earrings. She could hardly believe how easy it was and what an adrenaline rush she got when she made it outside and realized no one had seen her or followed her. A few weeks later, they decided to try it again at a different store. Before long, they were shoplifting every week. Lindsay was always the decoy, distracting the sales clerk's attention while Melissa slipped the item into her purse or pocket. It seemed harmless. They justified it by telling themselves that retail markup is like highway robbery anyway.

One weekend while they were shopping, they ran into Taylor in an exclusive designer clothing store and stopped to talk with her. Taylor explained that she was only looking. She dreamed of owning something—anything—from that store, but she couldn't afford it. Melissa asked if she would like to have something from the store for free, and Taylor said, "Yeah, right. Only in my dreams! Nothing in this store will ever be free."

Melissa said with a grin, "Meet me in the parking lot in about fifteen minutes."

Before Taylor had a chance to reply, Melissa winked at Lindsay and they went into action. Lindsay went to ask the nearest sales clerk a question while Melissa scoped out a silk tank and slipped it into her purse. Taylor was watching them, and when she realized what they were doing, she headed outside as quickly as she could. When Melissa and Lindsay joined her, they led her to their car and got inside. Then Melissa handed Taylor the silk tank.

"This is crazy! You just stole this!" Taylor said in disbelief.

"Yeah, it's easy!" Melissa said enthusiastically. "We do it all the time. Lindsay and I have a system. You should join us next time!"

Taylor was shocked, but at the same time she was excited by the thought of actually being able to wear the designer silk tank. "I couldn't do that, and I can't take this," she said.

"Sure you can!" Melissa said. "It's a gift. Taylor, it's so easy! And just think of all the great stuff you could get. I could show you how." In a strange way, the thought of getting Taylor to join them gave Melissa a rush like she'd had the first time she shoplifted.

Taylor felt terrible about keeping the tank, but she didn't want to offend Melissa. She had been so surprised that Melissa and Lindsay had stopped to talk to her, and she didn't want to blow the possibility of becoming friends.

Every day that week, Melissa made a point to speak to Taylor and invite her to "go shopping" with them sometime, but Taylor continued to say she couldn't do it. She still felt really guilty for having the tank Melissa had stolen. She hadn't been able to bring herself to wear it, but she admired it every day when she opened her closet. Every time she saw Melissa or Lindsay, she thought about being able to have some of the expensive things she couldn't afford. But she knew it would be wrong, so she kept pushing the thought out of her mind.

Several weeks later, Taylor had to run to a nearby store for something. It was going to be a quick trip — in and out. As she got out of her car, she couldn't believe what she saw. There were Melissa and Lindsay walking toward her in the parking lot, smiling and waving. Her heart skipped a beat and she felt sick. Never had she felt such a wrenching conflict within her. She seriously wondered if she would be able to stand her ground or if she would wind up giving in and joining them.

REAL QUESTIONS

Take a few minutes to answer the following questions. Then discuss them together.

1. Was there anything Nicole said in the video that really stood out to you?

2. Have you ever been in a tempting situation like Taylor? What is hard for you to say no to?

3. What makes it hard for you to say no?

4. Do you agree with the statement that "you are who you hang with"? Why or why not?

5. How much do your friends tend to influence the choices you make (what you wear, what you say, what you do)?

6. Has the desire to fit in or be accepted ever led you to make a bad decision? What happened? If you could have a do-over, what would you do differently?

7. Read Proverbs 6:27-28. How do these verses apply to tempting situations?

8. Have you ever thought you were strong in one area only to find yourself weak when actually tempted? Read Psalm 119:11, Matthew 26:41, and 1 Peter 5:8-9. What can we do to protect or guard ourselves against temptation?

9. What gives you the courage to take a stand and do what is right? Does 1 Corinthians 10:13 offer any encouragement for you?

KEEPING IT REAL
When Temptation Comes Calling

There's a saying about temptation: "Opportunity knocks once, but temptation leans on the doorbell." In other words, it's hard to ignore! Some temptations are extremely appealing and the struggle is intense from the start. Others seem to keep working on you over time, eating away at your defenses. In either case, if you're not prepared for temptation, you'll find it difficult to stand against it.

10. Describe a time when you found it difficult to stand against temptation.

Preparing for temptation may sound like a strange concept, but God's Word tells us that this is the very thing we must do if we want to overcome it. We are told to be alert, keep our guard up, pray for strength, give ourselves completely to God, hide God's Word in our hearts, stand firm, and look for a way out. In fact, we're assured that God will always provide a way out:

> God is faithful. He will not allow the temptation to be more than you can stand. When you are tempted, he will show you a way out so that you can endure. (1 Corinthians 10:13)

11. Describe a time when you were tempted and God showed you a way out. Did you take the escape He provided? If you could go back to that situation, would you do anything differently?

Taking a stand against temptation is worth the effort. In addition to helping us live as God wants us to live and protecting us from harm, it results in blessing! Just read what God's Word says about it: "God blesses those who patiently endure testing and temptation. Afterward they will receive the crown of life that God has promised to those who love him" (James 1:12).

12. Write a personal prayer to God, asking Him to help you take a stand against temptation.

REAL HOPE

Here are some suggestions to help guide your group prayer time. Be sure to share prayer concerns and pray for one another.

- Thank God for always providing a way out of temptation. Ask Him to give you the eyes to see the way out and the courage to take it.
- Pray for the wisdom to choose your friends wisely.
- Ask God to continually remind you that you can't play with fire without getting burned.
- Ask Him to help you stay alert and be on your guard against temptation.
- Pray for the strength to resist temptation and the courage to say no.
- Ask God to help you hide His Word in your heart so that you will not sin against Him.

Use the following space to write down prayer requests so you can pray for each other throughout the week.

REALITY CHECK

Tear out and post this page in a place you will see it often—a mirror, the refrigerator, your locker—or carry it in your pocket. You can also scan this QR code with your phone so you can take these verses and quotes with you wherever you go.

Week 6 Reality Check

Meditate on the following verses to nourish your thoughts with truth. Try to memorize one or more verses that stand out to you.

Be on your guard against temptation.

> Keep a cool head. Stay alert. The Devil is poised to pounce, and would like nothing better than to catch you napping. Keep your guard up. (1 Peter 5:8-9, MSG)

If you play with fire, you're going to get burned.

> Can you build a fire in your lap and not burn your pants? Can you walk barefoot on hot coals and not get blisters? (Proverbs 6:27-28, MSG)

You need God's help to overcome temptation.

> Stay awake and pray for strength against temptation. The spirit wants to do what is right, but the body is weak. (Matthew 26:41, NCV)

God will give you a way out of every temptation.

> If you think you are standing strong, be careful not to fall. The temptations in your life are no different from what others experience. And God is faithful. He will not allow the temptation to be more than you can stand. When you are tempted, he will show you a way out so that you can endure. (1 Corinthians 10:12-13)

You can resist temptation.

> Give yourselves completely to God. Stand against the devil, and the devil will run from you. (James 4:7, NCV)

> I have hidden your word in my heart, that I might not sin against you. (Psalm 119:11)

Enduring temptation brings blessing and reward.

> God blesses those who patiently endure testing and temptation. Afterward they will receive the crown of life that God has promised to those who love him. (James 1:12)

Every temptation is an opportunity to do good. — Rick Warren

WEEK 7

WAS IT MY FAULT?
FACING THE PAIN OF ABUSE

The truth will free you.

John 8:32, MSG

REAL LIFE. REAL ISSUES.

Begin by playing the group study video for week 7, "Was It My Fault?" (approximate running time: 7 minutes).

- Each year, 1 in 4 teens reports verbal, physical, emotional, or sexual abuse.[1]
- Approximately 1 in 4 girls is sexually abused by the age of 18.[2]
- Female victims of sexual abuse while in high school are more likely than others to have eating disorders, demonstrate suicidal behavior, get pregnant, or experiment with risky sex.[3]
- Approximately 1 in 5 high school girls has been abused by a dating partner either physically or sexually.[4]
- About 1 in 11 teens reports being a victim of physical dating violence.[5]

These are sobering statistics. If you haven't experienced abuse personally — whether it be verbal, physical, emotional, or sexual abuse — then the odds are high that someone you know has. It might even be a close friend. And more than likely, this friend has never told you about it. It's a secret she carries with her each day, and it's tearing her apart inside. Amber and Christie know what it's like to carry that kind of secret . . .

Amber is a very pretty girl, but she doesn't flaunt it. In fact, she's one of the nicest girls in school and is well-liked by just about everyone. She's a responsible daughter, a good student, and a devoted friend and girlfriend. She seems to have everything together.

Frankly, most of her friends are a little jealous of her — they want to be Amber most days. The thing even her closest friends don't know is that she's carrying a big secret. Her boyfriend, Josh, is very physical with her, and she fears he is becoming more abusive when they are together. Oh, and there's something else that may be important to know: Josh is the point guard on the basketball team, the homecoming king, and probably the most popular boy in school.

Amber has become afraid to be alone with Josh, especially if he has a bad game or is upset about something. He seems to like taking his frustrations out on her. At first he yelled at her and told her that whatever was bothering him at the time was her fault. Then he started becoming more physical with her, grabbing her arm and shoving her. Last week, after a particularly bad game, he slapped her, pushed her out of his car, and left her on the side of the road to walk home alone.

She doesn't know what to do or whether she should tell someone. Josh blames her for all kinds of things she doesn't think she had anything to do with, but she is pretty confused. Maybe Josh's reaction really is her fault in some way; maybe something she said or did made him angry. Who knows how boys think anyway? She wants to make him happy, and she likes the attention she gets by being with him at school. Who would believe her anyway? Josh is so popular that he could be with any girl he wanted. Maybe she should just accept the relationship for what it is and hope that Josh will get over his anger.

Meanwhile, Christie has an altogether different problem going on. You might say that Christie is the opposite of Amber. She is quiet, reads a lot, keeps to herself, and just hopes to get through every day without bothering anyone. She's nice enough but doesn't really have any friends to speak of. The problem is that recently a group of girls much cooler than she is have decided she doesn't belong in their space. They yell at her, push her around, take her books, just mean stuff. It started in the hallway near her locker, then it happened in the lunch room where everyone laughed about it. Later when she was walking home, they threw an orange at her from their car.

Most days Christie just hopes to get though the day without running into these mean girls, but they seem to always find her. The best part of the day for Christie is when she gets home and can be alone in her room with her books and cat. She is miserable and her fear is really starting to affect her physically. She is losing weight, her complexion is a mess, and she's afraid that next time these girls are going to beat her up.

Christie knows she needs to tell someone, but she doesn't have any friends to share this with and she believes her parents always exaggerate things. Christie is afraid that if she tells them, they'll charge up to the school, demand something be done, and whatever life she has at school will be over. But she knows she can't go on this way.

Both Amber and Christie go to the same church and are in the same youth group. Although they almost never talk with each other in the group, last week their youth pastor paired them up to share anything that might be bothering them. They both knew this was their chance to tell someone what was happing to them. As they began to share their stories, they found that others in the room were doing the same. Even though they didn't know each other well, Christie and Amber were surprised to find they both felt safe and accepted for who they are, weaknesses and all, after opening up. They began to feel like they didn't have to be alone in their secret struggles anymore.

REAL QUESTIONS

Take a few minutes to answer the following questions. Then discuss them together as a group.

1. Was there anything Nicole said that spoke to you this week? How about in the music video?

2. You just read a couple stories of two different kinds of abuse. Why do you think Amber and Christie waited so long to share their secrets?

3. Why do you think Amber felt that everything was her fault?

4. Has something painful happened to you that you feel was your fault?

5. Have you ever had a secret you needed to tell but were afraid to?

6. Do you ever feel that you are wearing a mask — being one way on the outside while you're dying on the inside? If so, why do you feel you must wear this mask?

7. When we think we can't tell anyone about something that has happened to us, such as bullying or abuse, there are usually fears keeping us silent. What might some of these fears be?

8. Behind the fears are lies. What might be the lies behind the fears you named?

9. Read John 8:32. Why is it important to make the truth known? What happens when we do?

10. Read Isaiah 61:3. What does this mean?

11. Read Romans 8:28. How did God bring good from Nicole Bromley's past of abuse and pain?

12. How has God brought good from a painful experience in your life or the life of someone you know?

13. Christie felt like she couldn't talk to her parents. Do you think her fears were realistic? Do you think her parents might have been able to help her in ways she didn't expect?

14. Where are some safe places you can turn when you are in need of help? List them here.

....

For resources and information about abuse or hotline numbers you can call, go to pages 119–120 of this book.

....

KEEPING IT REAL
Journaling Exercise

Consider the previous questions. Write a journal entry about how one or more of them may relate to your life. If you can't think of something personal, what about something that may have affected a friend or relative? Involve all of your senses as you journal, remembering specific sights, smells, sounds, or feelings you experienced at the time.

REAL HOPE

Here are some suggestions to help guide your group prayer time. Be sure to share prayer concerns and pray for one another.

- Ask God to help you identify any lies that have kept you silent about painful events or circumstances in your life, whether in the past or present.
- Ask God to give you the courage to take off your mask and be real with someone you can trust.
- Thank God for His promise that the truth will set you free.
- Pray for direction in seeking whatever help or guidance you may need.
- Ask God to set you free from the false guilt that whatever painful experiences have happened to you are your fault.
- Pray for deliverance from all fear.
- Thank God for His ability to bring good from bad experiences and circumstances, and ask Him to do this now in your life.

Use the following space to write down prayer requests so you can pray for each other throughout the week.

REALITY CHECK

Week 7 Reality Check

Tear out and post this page in a place you will see it often—a mirror, the refrigerator, your locker—or carry it in your pocket. You can also scan this QR code with your phone so you can take these verses and quotes with you wherever you go.

Meditate on the following verses to nourish your thoughts with truth. Try to memorize one or more verses that stand out to you.

Call on God when you're in need. He will help you.

> I am poor and needy; come quickly to me, O God. You are my help and my deliverer; Lord, do not delay. (Psalm 70:5, NIV)

> "I know the plans I have for you," says the Lord. "They are plans for good and not for disaster, to give you a future and a hope. In those days when you pray, I will listen. If you look for me wholeheartedly, you will find me. I will be found by you," says the Lord. "I will end your captivity and restore your fortunes. I will gather you out of the nations where I sent you and will bring you home again to your own land." (Jeremiah 29:11-14)

God's love will comfort you.

> The Lord your God is living among you. He is a mighty savior. He will take delight in you with gladness. With his love, he will calm all your fears. He will rejoice over you with joyful songs. (Zephaniah 3:17)

God can turn something ugly and painful into something beautiful.

> He will give a crown of beauty for ashes. (Isaiah 61:3)

Making the truth known brings freedom.

> The truth will free you. (John 8:32, MSG)

God promises to work all things for your good.

> We know that in everything God works for the good of those who love him. (Romans 8:28, NCV)

God promises to deliver you from your fears.

> I sought the Lord, and he answered me; he delivered me from all my fears. (Psalm 34:4, NIV)

> I am leaving you with a gift—peace of mind and heart. And the peace I give is a gift the world cannot give. So don't be troubled or afraid. (John 14:27)

> Be strong and courageous. Do not be afraid or terrified because of them, for the Lord your God goes with you; he will never leave you nor forsake you. (Deuteronomy 31:6, NIV)

> I am the Lord your God, who holds your right hand, and I tell you, "Don't be afraid. I will help you." (Isaiah 41:13, NCV)

I don't think of all the misery but of the beauty that still remains. —Anne Frank, *The Diary of a Young Girl*

WEEK 8

THE FUTURE YOU HOPE FOR
FINDING HOPE AND HEALING

I know what I'm doing. I have it all
planned out — plans to take care of
you, not abandon you, plans to
give you the future you hope for.

Jeremiah 29:11, MSG

REAL LIFE. REAL ISSUES.

Begin by playing the group study video for week 8, "The Future You Hope For" (approximate running time: 7 minutes).

Over the past seven weeks, we have taken a real and honest look at some of the pressures you face as a young woman in today's world. We also have helped you identify some of the lies that go hand in hand with these pressures—lies that keep you from experiencing the full and abundant life God has planned for you. One of the most dangerous lies of all is that there is no hope. It might sound something like this:

Things will never get better.
My situation is always going to be like this.
God can never forgive me.
I can never forgive him/her/them.
There's no way out of this.
I'll never be able to change.
It's hopeless.
I can never heal from this.

If you've ever had thoughts like these, listen carefully: There is always hope! You see, God is the Creator of new beginnings. God sent His Son, Jesus, to die and rise again so that you might have hope—the hope of forgiveness and restoration and new life. Because of Jesus, God wipes the slate of your life clean and offers you a brand-new start. He is in the business of making all things new; He is able to transform both you and your circumstances. There are so many influences in our lives that steal this hope from us by deceiving us and making us feel unworthy. But the truth is that nothing can separate you from God's miracle-working love!

It was this realization that changed everything for Amber and Christie. Even though they had been attending youth group for a long time (Amber to spend time with her friends and Christie because her parents expected her to go), neither girl knew what it was like to have a real relationship with God. But as the evening came to a close and their youth pastor called them back together as a group, he began to explain that Jesus had been willing to give up everything and to suffer and die so that every person could have a brand-new life.

She'd heard talks like this before, but Christie felt like she was hearing it for the first time. She had never felt so excited to know that she could actually wipe the slate of her life completely clean and start over. Jesus gave His life so that she could be right with God and made new, and He wanted to know her and have a relationship with her. She didn't have to be alone, and she felt truly wanted and loved.

Sitting next to Christie, Amber began to realize that she didn't have to keep trying to be perfect — the perfect student, perfect friend, perfect girlfriend. She could never earn Jesus' love, because He already loved her just the way she was. All she had to do was surrender all of her pressures to Him and trust Him with her future. She finally felt free from the stress of trying to do and be everything.

At the closing of his talk, the pastor invited people to come forward to pray, and Amber and Christie turned to each other with tears running down their cheeks. As they knelt together and prayed, others began to join them one by one, placing their arms around them in one giant hug. For the first time in their lives, Christie and Amber knew they were loved. They sensed deep within that even if they shared their secrets, this circle of friends would still love and accept them.

As the night ended, they knew it was time to stand up against the abuse they'd been experiencing. It wasn't going to be easy getting over all the pain or facing those who had hurt them, but Amber and Christie knew Jesus would be with them and help them every step of the way. Ahead was a life filled with hope.

REAL QUESTIONS

Take a few minutes to answer the following questions. Then discuss them together.

1. What are you hoping for?

2. When was a time in your life when you failed, made a mistake, or "fell short"? How did the experience make you feel?

3. When we heard Dana's story in the film, she encouraged us to look up when we don't know where to go or who to turn to. What does it mean to "look up" after you fall, and why is this important? What are some things that can keep you from looking up?

4. Read Psalm 121:2. What are some practical ways you can "look up" to God for help?

5. Read 2 Corinthians 5:17. What does this verse promise? What hope does it give you for the present? For the future?

6. Read Colossians 3:12-14. According to these verses, why are we to forgive others? Why do you think forgiveness is an important part of the healing process? Does forgiveness mean that we must excuse or forget the wrong others have done? Explain your answers.

7. How would you describe or explain God's grace? What does it mean to give grace to others?

8. What is one way you have given grace to someone? How has someone else given grace to you?

9. What does it mean to "walk with others" on life's journey? Why is this important?

10. How have others helped you find hope or healing (for example, through their stories, encouragement, or support)?

11. What does it mean to be used by God (see 2 Corinthians 1:3-7)? How might God use you—and all you've been through—to help others find hope?

12. Read Romans 15:13. According to this verse, what is the key to being filled with hope? What do you need to trust God for right now?

KEEPING IT REAL
Cardboard Testimonies

Most of us love a good makeover. Whether it's in the pages of a magazine or on our TV screens, we're captivated by the idea of taking someone or something and remaking it so that it looks "new and improved." That's what makes shows like *What Not to Wear* and *Extreme Makeover: Home Edition* so popular.

13. What appeals to you about the concept of a makeover? Make a quick list here.

You might say that God is the Master Makeover Artist. The Bible tells us that God is in the business of making all things new, including you and me. "Anyone who belongs to Christ has become a new person. The old life is gone; a new life has begun!" (2 Corinthians 5:17). The New Century Version says that "the old things have gone; everything is made new!" The idea that God can make everything new gives us great hope!

When we give our lives to Jesus—along with all the problems and messes that are part of our lives—He can make them into something new and beautiful. But He won't take them from us; we have to surrender them.

Would you like to surrender your life to Jesus in exchange for a new life full of hope? Write a prayer expressing your desire to surrender—or recommit—your life to Him and to trust Him now. If you're not sure what it means to surrender your life to Jesus, take this time to read more about it on pages 115–118.

Surrender involves trust. God wants you to trust Him. He wants you to be confident that He has good plans for you. We've read this verse multiple times over the past few weeks, and that's because it's one we hope you will remember and internalize: "I know what I'm doing. I have it all planned out—plans to take care of you, not abandon you, plans to give you the future you hope for" (Jeremiah 29:11, MSG).

What is the future you hope for? Tell God about your hopes and dreams. You can either list them here or on a piece of paper or in a notebook. This can be a great way to keep track of things to pray for. Later you can write down how God is working through your life, fulfilling your dreams, and answering your prayers!

If you will believe God's promise that He has good plans for you, and if you will trust God to work out those plans in His time and in His way, you will be filled with peace, joy, and hope. And there is nothing you can't overcome when your life is filled with the peace, joy, and hope of God!

People sometimes use cardboard testimonies as a powerful way to express the hope of new life in Jesus Christ. On one side of the cardboard, they write a few words to describe what life was like before finding hope in Jesus, and on the other side, they describe what life is like after experiencing the hope and new life He gives. What would your cardboard testimony be?

My life before finding hope in Jesus:

My life after finding hope in Jesus:

REAL HOPE

Here are some suggestions to help guide your group prayer time. Be sure to share prayer concerns and pray for one another.

- Thank God for giving His Son, Jesus Christ, so that we might have the hope of new life.
- Thank God for His amazing grace and forgiveness, which give us second chances, and pray to be able to extend this same grace and forgiveness to others.
- Thank God for His good plans for you — plans for a future filled with hope.
- Praise God for His ability to make all things new (people, situations, and circumstances).
- Ask God to help you trust Him so that you may be filled with joy, peace, and hope.
- Thank God that He's always with you, ready to help.
- Pray for the ability to keep your eyes focused on how big your God is, not how big your problems are.

Use the following space to write down prayer requests so you can pray for each other throughout the week.

REALITY CHECK

Tear out and post this page in a place you will see it often—a mirror, the refrigerator, your locker—or carry it in your pocket. You can also scan this QR code with your phone so you can take these verses and quotes with you wherever you go.

Meditate on the following verses to nourish your thoughts with truth. Try to memorize one or more verses that stand out to you.

Week 8 Reality Check

BELIEF + TRUST = PEACE, JOY, HOPE

God has good plans for you.

I know what I'm doing. I have it all planned out—plans to take care of you, not abandon you, plans to give you the future you hope for. (Jeremiah 29:11, MSG)

God makes all things new.

Anyone who belongs to Christ has become a new person. The old life is gone; a new life has begun! (2 Corinthians 5:17)

Behold, I am making all things new. (Revelation 21:5, NASB)

You can count on God.

I'm not giving up. I'm sticking around to see what God will do. I'm waiting for God to make things right. I'm counting on God to listen to me. (Micah 7:7, MSG)

As you trust in God, you will be filled with hope.

I pray that God, the source of hope, will fill you completely with joy and peace because you trust in him. Then you will overflow with confident hope through the power of the Holy Spirit. (Romans 15:13)

God is the source of your help.

I lift up my eyes to the mountains—where does my help come from? My help comes from the LORD, the Maker of heaven and earth. (Psalm 121:1-2, NIV)

God is our refuge and strength, always ready to help in times of trouble. (Psalm 46:1)

Expect to have hope rekindled. Expect your prayers to be answered in wondrous ways. The dry seasons in life do not last. The spring rains will come again. —Sarah Ban Breathnach

REAL-LIFE PROFILES

The girls whose stories are profiled in the *Yellow Roses* study have life experiences that you are likely to identify with on some level. They are dealing with a variety of life and relationship issues similar to those you or your friends may be dealing with as well. You can meet them and get to know a little about them in the following profiles.

LINDSAY

Lindsay is pretty and popular. Her mom and dad divorced when she was in elementary school, and she's insecure about fitting in, despite her popularity. She feels she has to be perfect in order to be liked and accepted. She's consumed with looking at herself in the mirror and is constantly checking her hair and makeup. Lindsay is very interested in guys but doesn't have a clue that her preoccupation with herself is a real turnoff. Sometimes her self-absorption causes her to be petty and careless with her words. At times when she is feeling especially insecure, she can even be cruel, which has given her the reputation of a "mean girl" among the less popular crowd. She has a hard time thinking of others because she is so concerned about herself and her image.

MELISSA

Melissa's parents divorced when she was just a baby, and her father has never been very involved in her life. She sees him at Christmas and spends one week with him in the summer. Her mother is a self-made, successful businesswoman who has little time for Melissa and who showers her with money and things to make up for it. Melissa often spends the money her mom gives her on her friends, especially Lindsay. They like to go shopping together. Melissa longs for attention and will do just about anything to get it. She likes to party and isn't afraid of taking risks. In fact, she likes the rush it gives her. She's on the dance team, but the coach has warned her that if the rumors about her partying are true, she might get suspended from the team. Melissa could be an outstanding student, but she thinks it's not cool to be smart, so she doesn't apply herself.

TOMIKA

Tomika has never known her father; it has always been just her and her mother. She's outgoing and flirty with the guys and loves to talk. She tends to think out loud, and she doesn't realize that constantly talking about everything that's going on in her life often comes off as either complaining or neediness, which turns people away from her. She also tends to be a little controlling. Lately she has been hanging out with Derrick. She lets Derrick take her out and show her a good time as a "friend with benefits," but secretly she's hoping it will become something more. She's longing for love, and she thinks she may have found it with Derrick.

SARAH

Sarah is pretty and smart. She's also a talented basketball player who is being considered for a basketball scholarship. Sarah attends church fairly regularly with her parents but is struggling to have a real relationship with Jesus. To others, she seems to have it all, but she's nearing her breaking point under all the pressure. Her parents run their own business, a gift shop, and expect her to help out as much as possible despite her demanding schedule. They also have high expectations of her regarding academics and college scholarships. Her father has always pushed her to excel athletically as well. Her boyfriend, Matt (also an athlete), is pressuring her to have sex, and even though she knows it would be wrong, it's getting harder and harder to say no. The truth is that she's afraid of losing him.

CASSIE

Cassie and Sarah have been best friends since elementary school. Cassie is average in every way and easygoing. Her carefree attitude is something that helps her cope with stress. She jokes a lot and tries to be the one who makes everything okay among her friends. She has stress and pressure in her life like everyone else, but she relies upon her Christian faith and her relationship with Jesus Christ for strength and hope. Cassie struggles with feelings of insecurity and sometimes wishes she was more beautiful, smart, and popular, but then she reminds herself that God made her just the way she is for a reason. She has an older sister, whom she adores. Cassie is excited about the future and looks forward to pursuing the great plans God has in store for her.

TAYLOR

Taylor is five foot five and slightly underweight for her age. Her boyfriend, Michael, wonders how she can eat so much junk food and not put on weight. She hides her binge eating and purging so well that no one—not even Michael or her parents—is on to her. Taylor likes to read fashion magazines and dreams of being a model. If only she were taller—and thinner. Taylor's never satisfied with her looks and wants to have plastic surgery someday. She wishes people paid more attention to her. As the middle child, with an older brother and a younger sister, she wishes she got more attention at home, too. Because of her brother's involvement in several sports and her sister's ongoing health issues, Taylor often feels ignored and alone, so she spends most of her time with Michael, who has image issues of his own. They've known each other since elementary school and go to the same church.

KRISTA

Krista lives to dance—that is, she *lived* to dance. Dance was her life until her dance teacher crushed her dream of dancing professionally when she carelessly remarked that Krista would never have the body of a professional dancer. After that, Krista's self-esteem took a nosedive and she slowly slipped into depression, withdrawing from family and friends and even dance. Now she struggles with body image and is trying desperately to lose weight. Her depression and aloofness also have made her the target of cruelty and "mean girl" bullying.

AMBER

Amber is sixteen and very pretty, but she doesn't flaunt it. In fact, she's one of the nicest girls at school, and just about everyone who knows her likes her. She's a member of the National Honor Society and president of the student council. Amber tries to do everything right—be a good daughter, good student, good friend and girl-friend—but she can't help wondering if everyone likes her only for who she is on the outside. She also has a secret about her boyfriend, Josh, that no one knows about, and she's afraid of what would happen if she told. She longs to know that she's truly loved and accepted for who she really is, not just what she does.

CHRISTIE

Christie is a nice girl, but she's pretty shy and no one really knows her, not even the kids at youth group. In fact, Christie would probably say that her best friend is her cat, Mittens. She often goes home after school and uses her books as an escape from the real world of mean girls and loneliness. Christie knows that her parents love her, but she feels like sometimes they show it by getting too involved in her problems. Instead of talking to them about the bullying she's experiencing at school, she's bottled up all of her feelings to the point that she doesn't feel she can continue dealing with the pain. She wishes there was just one other person who knew how hard it is for her to go to school every day.

KIMBERLY

Kimberly's life isn't the same now that her boyfriend has broken up with her. She dated several guys before him, and everyone knows she just isn't happy without a guy in her life. Kimberly believes that if only she could find the right guy, her life would be complete. She is envious of her friends who have boyfriends, and she feels that she needs to find someone soon. As far as she is concerned, being "single" is a complete waste. After a while, Kimberly starts seeing Carlos, and their relationship quickly moves to being very physical.

RESOURCES
TRUSTING JESUS

THE BRIDGE TO LIFE

Step 1 — God's Love and His Plan

God created us in His own image to be His friend and to experience a full life assured of His love, abundant and eternal.

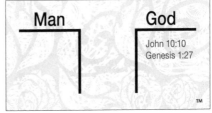

- Jesus said, "I have come that they may have life, and have it to the full." (John 10:10, NIV)
- We have peace with God through our Lord Jesus Christ. (Romans 5:1, NIV)

God planned for us to have peace and abundant life right now, so why are most people not having this experience?

Step 2 — Our Problem: Separation from God

God created us in His own image to have abundant (meaningful) life. He did not make us robots to automatically love and obey Him, but He gave us a will and freedom of choice. We chose to disobey God and go our own willful way. We still make this choice today. This results in separation from God.

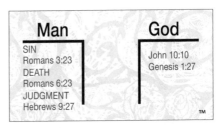

- All have sinned and fall short of the glory of God. (Romans 3:23, NIV)
- Your iniquities have separated you from your God; your sins have hidden his face from you, so that he will not hear. (Isaiah 59:2, NIV)

On our own, there's no way we can attain the perfection needed to bridge the gap to God. Through the ages, individuals have tried many ways, without success. Good works won't do it (or religion or money or morality or philosophy).

- There is a way that appears to be right, but in the end it leads to death. (Proverbs 14:12, NIV)

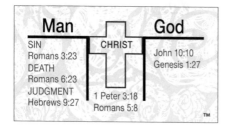

Step 3 — God's Remedy: The Cross

Jesus Christ is the only answer to this problem. He died on the cross and rose from the grave, paying the penalty for our sin and bridging the gap between God and people.

- Christ also suffered once for sins, the righteous for the unrighteous, to bring you to God. (1 Peter 3:18, NIV)
- There is one God and one mediator between God and mankind, the man Christ Jesus. (1 Timothy 2:5, NIV)
- God demonstrates his own love for us in this: While we were still sinners, Christ died for us. (Romans 5:8, NIV)

Step 4 — Our Response

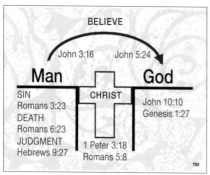

Believing means trust and commitment: acknowledging our sinfulness, trusting Christ's forgiveness, and letting Him control our lives. Eternal, abundant life is a gift for us to receive.

- God so loved the world that he gave his one and only Son, that whoever believes in him shall not perish but have eternal life. (John 3:16, NIV)
- Very truly I tell you, whoever hears my word and believes him who sent me has eternal life and will

not be judged but has crossed over from death to
life. (John 5:24, NIV)

Is there any reason why you should not cross over to
God's side and be certain of eternal life?

How to Receive Christ

1. Admit your need (that you are a sinner).
2. Be willing to turn from your sins (repent).
3. Believe that Jesus Christ died on the cross to pay the
   penalty for your sins and rose from the grave.
4. Through prayer, invite Jesus Christ to come in and control your life through the Holy Spirit (receive Him as
   Lord and Savior of your life).

What to Pray

Dear Lord Jesus, I know I am a sinner and need Your forgiveness. I know I deserve to be punished for my sins, and I
believe that You died to pay that price and rose from the
grave. I want to turn from my sins. I now invite You to
come into my heart and life. I want to trust and follow You
as the Lord and Savior of my life. Thank You for Your forgiveness and the everlasting life I now have. Amen.

God's Assurance of Eternal Life

If you've prayed this prayer and are trusting Christ, the
Bible says you can be sure you have eternal life.

- Everyone who calls on the name of the Lord will be
  saved. (Romans 10:13, NIV)
- It is by grace you have been saved, through
  faith — and this is not from yourselves, it is the gift
  of God — not by works, so that no one can boast.
  (Ephesians 2:8-9, NIV)

- Whoever has the Son has life; whoever does not have the Son of God does not have life. I write these things to you who believe in the name of the Son of God so that you may know that you have eternal life. (1 John 5:12-13, NIV)

Receiving Christ, we are born into God's family through the supernatural work of the Holy Spirit, who indwells every believer. This is called regeneration, or the "new birth."

WHAT NEXT?

This is just the beginning of a wonderful new life in Christ. To deepen this relationship, you should:

1. Maintain regular intake of the Bible to know Christ better.
2. Talk to God every day in prayer.
3. Tell others about your new faith in Christ.
4. Worship, live in community, and serve with other Christians in a church where Christ is preached.
5. As Christ's representative in a needy world, demonstrate your new life by your love and concern for others.[1]

HELPING VICTIMS OF ABUSE

If you or someone you know is being abused, it's important to tell a trusted adult who can help you. If you do not feel safe talking to your parents or another adult, there are organizations that can help you.

Be safe! Computer use can be monitored and is impossible to completely clear. Cell phones can also be monitored. If you are afraid your phone, Internet, or computer usage might be monitored, please use a safer computer or phone to call your local hotline or a national hotline.

For immediate medical or police assistance, call 911.

NATIONAL DATING ABUSE HOTLINE

Loveisrespect.org is a resource that can provide a safe place to access information and help you determine whether or not a relationship is abusive as well as report abuse while ensuring confidentiality.[2]

Peer advocates are available for assistance and support twenty-four hours a day, seven days a week:

National Dating
Abuse Hotline

- Website: www.loveisrespect.org (live chat available)
- Phone: 1-866-331-9474 or 1-866-331-8453 TTY
- Text: "loveis" to 77054
- E-mail available through contact page

NATIONAL DOMESTIC VIOLENCE HOTLINE

The National Domestic Violence Hotline creates access by providing support through advocacy, safety planning, resources, and hope to everyone affected by domestic violence.[3]

National Domestic
Violence Hotline

Assistance is available twenty-four hours a day, seven days a week:

- Website: www.thehotline.org
- Phone: 1-800-799-SAFE (7233) or 1-800-787-3224 TTY
- E-mail available through contact page

CHILDHELP NATIONAL CHILD ABUSE HOTLINE

The Childhelp National Child Abuse Hotline is dedicated to the prevention of child abuse. Serving the United States, its territories, and Canada, the hotline is staffed with professional crisis counselors who, through interpreters, can provide assistance in 170 languages. The hotline offers crisis intervention, information, literature, and referrals to thousands of emergency, social service, and support resources. All calls are anonymous and confidential.[4]

Assistance is available twenty-four hours a day, seven days a week:

- Website: www.childhelp.org
- Phone: 1-800-4-A-CHILD (422-4453)

National Child
Abuse Hotline

NOTES

Week 2: Too Much Pressure!
1. Stephen Hinshaw, *The Triple Bind* (New York: Ballantine Books, 2009), x.

Week 3: Airbrushed Illusions
1. "Body Image and Nutrition: Fast Facts," *Teen Health and the Media*, http://depts.washington.edu/thmedia/.
2. "Eating Disorders Statistics," *National Association of Anorexia Nervosa and Associated Disorders, Inc.,* http://www.anad.org/get-information/about-eating-disorders/eating-disorders-statistics/.
3. Stephen Hinshaw, *The Triple Bind* (New York: Ballantine Books, 2009), xi.
4. "Quick Facts," *Women Against the Media's Portrayal of Women*, 2010, http://www.wampow.org/?title=Quick Facts.
5. "Teenagers and Cosmetic (Aesthetic) Plastic Surgery," *American Society for Aesthetic Plastic Surgery*, http://www.surgery.org/media/news-releases/teenagers-and-cosmetic-aesthetic-plastic-surgery.
6. Everlife, "What's Beautiful," released January 6, 2010, Independent.

Week 5: stix n stones
1. Stephen Hinshaw, *The Triple Bind* (New York: Ballantine Books, 2009), 134.

Week 7: Was It My Fault?
1. "Dating Violence Facts," *Centers for Disease Control and Prevention*, March 5, 2010, http://www.cdc.gov/chooserespect/understandingdatingviolence/datingviolencefacts.html.
2. "Sexual Abuse Statistics," Teen Help.com, http://www.teenhelp.com/teen-abuse/sexual-abuse-stats.html.
3. "Sexual Abuse Statistics."

4. "Dating Violence Facts," *Centers for Disease Control and Prevention*, March 5, 2010, http://www.cdc.gov/chooserespect/understandingdatingviolence/datingviolencefacts.html.

5. "Dating Violence Facts."

Resources

1. The Navigators, "The Bridge to Life," 2011, www.navigators.org/us/resources/illustrations/items/The%20Bridge%20to%20Life.

2. LoveIsRespect.org.

3. *The Hotline*, www.thehotline.org.

4. *Childhelp*, www.childhelp.org.

Complete your Bible-study experience with more from *Yellow Roses.*

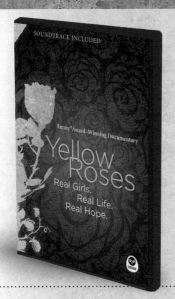

Yellow Roses Documentary
Mike Edwards and Larry Mead

This Emmy award–winning documentary is filled with heart-wrenching stories of young girls as well as the promise of a beautiful new beginning these girls can have. By combining this full-length documentary film and a video-based Bible study, *Yellow Roses* introduces a refreshing, unique approach to ministry with young women that encourages open, honest sharing about the real issues they deal with on a daily basis.

978-1-61291-167-0

Yellow Roses DVD Leader's Kit
Mike Edwards and Larry Mead

Young girls today are faced with a lot — peer pressure, having the perfect boyfriend, being popular, body image — but where can they go to talk honestly with others about these pressures? *Yellow Roses* is about real girls telling their true stories about themselves and offering hope to others. Best with the student workbook, this kit includes the full-length Emmy award–winning documentary, seven video segments, the original soundtrack, and a leader's guide.

978-1-61291-166-3

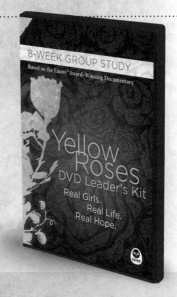

To order copies, call NavPress at **1-800-366-7788**
or log on to **www.NavPress.com**.

NAVPRESS
Discipleship Inside Out®

MY LIFE IS **TOUGHER** THAN MOST **PEOPLE REALIZE.**

I TRY TO KEEP EVERYTHING IN BALANCE: FRIENDS, FAMILY, WORK, SCHOOL, AND GOD.

IT'S NOT EASY.

I KNOW WHAT MY PARENTS BELIEVE AND WHAT MY PASTOR SAYS.

BUT IT'S NOT ABOUT THEM. IT'S ABOUT ME...

ISN'T IT TIME I OWN MY FAITH?

THROUGH THICK AND THIN, KEEP YOUR HEARTS AT ATTENTION, IN ADORATION BEFORE CHRIST, YOUR MASTER. BE READY TO SPEAK UP AND TELL ANYONE WHO ASKS WHY YOU'RE LIVING THE WAY YOU ARE, AND ALWAYS WITH THE UTMOST COURTESY. 1 PETER 3:15 (MSG)

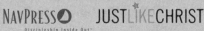